weblinks

You don't need a computer to use this book. But, for readers who do have access to the Internet, the book provides links to recommended websites which offer additional information and resources on the subject.

You will find weblinks boxes like this on some pages of the book.

weblinks

For more information about the death penalty go to www.waylinks.co.uk /EthicalDebates/deathpenalty

waylinks.co.uk

To help you find the recommended websites easily and quickly, weblinks are provided on our own website, **waylinks.co.uk.** These take you straight to the relevant websites and save you typing in the Internet address yourself.

Internet safety

↗ Never give out personal details, which include: your name, address, school, telephone number, email address, password and mobile number.

↗ Do not respond to messages which make you feel uncomfortable – tell an adult.

↗ Do not arrange to meet in person someone you have met on the Internet.

↗ Never send your picture or anything else to an online friend without a parent's or teacher's permission.

↗ If you see anything that worries you, tell an adult.

A note to adults
Internet use by children should be supervised. We recommend that you install filtering software which blocks unsuitable material.

Website content

The weblinks for this book are checked and updated regularly. However, because of the nature of the Internet, the content of a website may change at any time, or a website may close down without notice. While the Publishers regret any inconvenience this may cause readers, they cannot be responsible for the content of any website other than their own.

ETHICAL

DEBATES

The Death Penalty

KAYE STEARMAN

WAYLAND

First published in 2007 by Wayland

Reprinted in 2007

Copyright © Wayland 2007

Wayland
338 Euston Road
London NW1 3BH

Wayland Australia
Level 17/207 Kent Street
Sydney, NSW 2000

Editor: Patience Coster
Series Editor: Camilla Lloyd
Consultant: Emily Bolton
Designer: Rita Storey
Picture Researcher: Diana Morris

Picture Acknowledgments: The author and publisher would like to thank the following for allowing their pictures to be reproduced in this publication:
Cover photograph: Guard escorting prisoner, Greg Smith/Corbis
Rolex de la Pena/epa/Corbis: 1, 28, David Zentz/AP/Empics: 4, map Ian Thompson, STR/AFP/Getty Images: 7, Greg Smith/Corbis: front cover, 8, Art Media/HIP/Topfoto: 9, J. A. Hampton/Topical Press Agency/Getty Images: 10, Farjana K. Godhuly/AFP/Getty Images: 11, Michael Freeman/Corbis: 12, Roger-Viollet/Topfoto: 13, Mary Evans PL: 14, 24, Chaiwat Subprasom/Reuters/Corbis 15, Radu Sigheti/Reuters/Corbis: 16, Rex Features: 17, Topfoto: 18, 40, John Gress/Reuters/Corbis: 19, David Leeson/ Dallas Morning News / The Image Works/Topfoto: 20, 25, RS/Keystone USA/Rex Features: 21, US District Court/ Handout/ epa/ Corbis: 22, Sophie Elbaz/Sygma/Corbis: 26, Lefteris Pitarakis/AP/Empics: 27, B.R. Neilson/Rex Features: 30, Ted Soqui/Corbis: 32, Manan_ Vatsyayana/AFP/Getty Images: 34, AFP/Getty Images: 35, Luis Enrique Ascui/Reuters/Corbis: 37, Universal Pictorial Press Photo/Topfoto: 38, Jana Birchum/ The Image Works/Topfoto: 41, Steven Georges/Press-Telegram/Corbis: 42, Reuters/Corbis: 43, Jamal Saidi/Reuters/Corbis: 45.

British Library Cataloguing in Publication Data:

Stearman, Kaye
  The death penalty. - (Ethical debates)
  1. Capital punishment - Moral and ethical aspects -
  Juvenile literature
I. Title
179.7

ISBN-13: 978 0 7502 5024 5

Printed in China

Wayland is a division of Hachette Children's Books, an Hachette Livre UK Company

contents

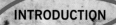

Real-life case study

This real-life case study highlights some of the issues that surround the debate on the death penalty.

case study

Larry Bright

Larry Bright is a serial killer. In just 15 months, between July 2003 and October 2004, he murdered eight women, burned their bodies and dumped their charred remains. At first, the police in Peoria, Illinois, USA, appeared uninterested, perhaps because the victims were poor black women, and several were drug users and prostitutes. However, a community outcry forced the police to act, and Bright was tracked down, arrested and charged with murder.

When the trial opened in 2005, the prosecutors asked for the death penalty to be given as a sentence. Illinois had operated a moratorium on executions since 2000, but the punishment was still available and Bright's crimes were especially terrible. Although Bright had already confessed and wanted to plead guilty, he was persuaded to plead not guilty. The not guilty plea meant that the trial would be a long and difficult one, especially for the victims' families who would have to endure months of testimony.

In May 2006, the court and the victims' families came to an agreement. If Bright pleaded guilty, he would not receive the death penalty. Instead, he would serve a life sentence in a maximum-security prison, without parole and with no right to appeal. Not everyone agreed that this was the right course. One of Bright's victims was Brenda Erving. Her daughter, Cynthia, supported the agreement, saying: 'He's not going to make it in jail either way. He's going to die there.' Mrs Erving's other daughter, Tyrahonda, wanted the death penalty: 'His family can still go and see him, he took that from us. I feel that they should have taken his life like he did theirs. He didn't give them a choice, so why give him one?'

Linda Neal was another victim. Her father, Harrison Neal, said: 'I didn't want to see him get the death penalty because I don't want to see nobody die.... Just as long as he's off the streets.' Her brother, Kevin, expressed his sorrow that Bright had never acknowledged the pain he had caused: 'That 20 seconds of saying he was sorry wasn't good enough for me.'

Before handing down the life sentence, Judge James Shadid told Bright that the victims' families had shown 'more consideration, more mercy and more respect for your life than you showed them for theirs.'

It's a fact

In 2005, 81 countries sponsored a United Nations resolution calling for a worldwide moratorium on executions.

viewpoints

'Punishments are imposed on a person, not on racial or economic groups. Guilt is personal. The only relevant question is: does the person to be executed deserve the punishment?'
Ernest van den Haag, Professor of Jurisprudence, Fordham University

'The death penalty is essentially an arbitrary punishment. This lack of objective, measurable standards ensures that the application of the death penalty will be discriminatory against racial, gender, and ethnic groups.'
Reverend Jesse Jackson, religious leader and politician

◀ Kevin Armstrong, the brother of one of Larry Bright's victims, is interviewed by the press following Bright's not guilty plea on 30 May 2006. The death penalty is an issue that can divide the families of murder victims, who must relive their pain and suffering at the trial and in front of the media.

CHAPTER 1

What is the death penalty?

The death penalty is when the government takes a person's life as a punishment for wrongdoing. The legal term is 'capital punishment'. The word 'capital' comes from the Latin word, *caput*, meaning 'head' – lose your head and you lose your life.

The death penalty is the most extreme punishment a government can use on its citizens. It has been used at different times in many societies in all parts of the world, although mainly as a last resort in a small number of cases. At the beginning of the twentieth century, almost all countries practised some form of capital punishment, but it is no longer used in many countries.

The pros and cons of the death penalty are widely debated. Can it ever be justified? If it can, under what circumstances should it be used? Does the death penalty act as a deterrent? What are the alternatives? Does it contribute to a safe and secure society?

This table shows the number of executions carried out in 2005.

Country	Executions	
China	1,770	*
Iran	94	*
Saudi Arabia	86	*
USA	60	

* Estimates – the true figures are probably much higher.
Source: Amnesty International Report 2006

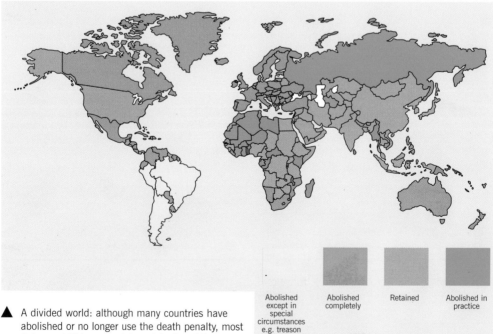

Abolished except in special circumstances e.g. treason	Abolished completely	Retained	Abolished in practice

▲ A divided world: although many countries have abolished or no longer use the death penalty, most Asian and African countries retain (keep) it.

Supporters say that governments must keep the death penalty because it is the only appropriate and effective punishment for certain crimes. They say that its use stops future crimes by executing violent offenders. They also argue that it deters other criminals, brings relief to victims and, overall, makes society safer for everyone.

Opponents say the death penalty is state-sponsored killing and that it has no place in a modern society. In addition, they argue that it is a cruel and painful punishment, used in unfair or discriminatory ways; it is also subject to error and can never be reversed. They believe it has no value as a deterrent, does not help the families of victims and, in general, leads to a more violent and less humane society.

The death penalty today

By 2006, 86 countries had abolished the death penalty for all offences, and 11 for all offences except under special circumstances (such as treason). Another 25 countries had not used the death penalty for ten years or more. However, 74 countries (accounting for 86 per cent of the world's population) retained use of the death penalty (see map opposite).

Countries in Europe, Latin America, southern Africa and the Pacific no longer use the death penalty. It has also been abolished in Canada. Most countries in Asia and Africa, the Caribbean and the USA retain it. Most death penalty countries are poor and undemocratic. Only two rich, democratic countries – the USA and Japan – retain the death penalty.

There are no reliable estimates of the numbers of executions because many are carried out in secrecy, unreported by governments or the media. According to the human rights organization, Amnesty International, at least 2,148 people were executed in 2005, another 5,186 were sentenced to death, and around 20,000 remained on death row worldwide (see page 8). Just four countries – China, Iran, Saudi Arabia and the USA – accounted for 94 per cent of executions (see table opposite).

▼ In 2004, in the Chinese city of Wenzhou, police present a group of convicts for sentencing. China executes a large number of people, but today the practice is coming under criticism.

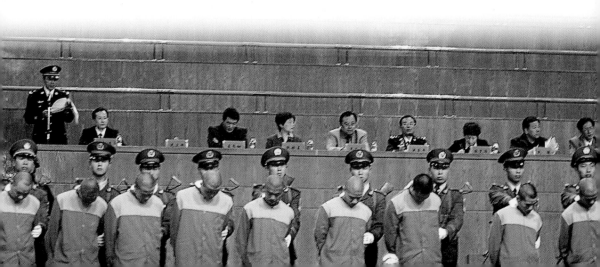

▲ Guards with an inmate at a prison in Texas. Most democratic countries no longer use the death penalty, but it is still used by many US states, especially those in the south.

The US situation

Apart from a brief period between 1972 and 1976, the death penalty has been in continuous use in the USA, although the situation varies between states. In 2006, 38 of the 51 states, plus the federal government and US military, retained the death penalty, although five states had not executed anyone since 1976. Twelve states, plus the District of Columbia (Washington), do not have a death penalty. Since 1976 there have been more than 1,000 executions. Texas has the highest number, with one-third of the executions,

followed by Virginia, Oklahoma, Missouri and Florida. More than 3,000 people remain on death row (a section of prison for those awaiting execution), and some have been there for 20 years or more.

The death penalty in history

The death penalty has been used in many different societies throughout history, along with other punishments such as beatings and amputation of limbs, sending a wrongdoer into exile or slavery, or paying compensation to the victim's family. The death penalty was generally reserved for the worst crimes, such as murder, rape or kidnapping, but sometimes it was given for relatively minor offences, such as stealing.

Ancient civilizations, including the Egyptians, Assyrians, Babylonians, Greeks and Romans, developed penal codes, with the death penalty as an ultimate sanction. When the Greek philosopher, Draco, wrote a new penal code in 621 BC, it was so severe that it gave us the word 'draconian'

meaning 'excessively harsh'. Later, the Christian churches and Islamic authorities developed codes that included the death penalty, but also recognized exceptional cases and alternative punishments. A rare exception was the Tang Dynasty in China, which banned the death penalty for twelve years between AD 747 and 759.

viewpoints

'And Draco himself, they say, being asked why he made death the penalty for most offences, replied that in his opinion the lesser ones deserved it, and for the greater ones no heavier penalty could be found.'
Plutarch (Greek historian), *Life of Solon*, written in the first century AD

'In giving man the example of cruelty, the death penalty is for society one more evil.... The death penalty is not a right but a war of the state against the citizen.'
Cesare Beccaria, *On Crimes and Punishments*, 1764

It's a fact

According to the United Nations, the highest per capita use of the death penalty is in Singapore, with a rate of 13.57 executions per one million population for the period 1994-99.

▼ The death penalty has been used throughout history. This picture, dating from the thirteenth century, is of the King of Kashmir watching a beheading by sword.

The abolition movement begins

The movement to abolish the death penalty is a fairly recent one. It began slowly, arising from the European 'Enlightenment' in the eighteenth century which laid the basis for modern ideas of citizenship and human rights. In 1764 an Italian aristocrat, Cesare Beccaria, published his book *On Crimes and Punishments*, which argued that the death penalty and state torture were unjust and did not benefit society. Swayed by these arguments, in 1786 Grand Duke Leopold abolished capital punishment in Tuscany.

Other states were slow to follow, although many limited the crimes for which the death penalty could be imposed, stopped public executions and tried to develop more 'humane' methods of execution.

Since that time, governments have developed many codes and scales of punishment. In general, these have limited the death penalty to punishing the severest crimes or they have abolished it, replacing it with long-term imprisonment in jails and asylums for the mentally ill. The imprisonment 'solution' combines punishment, deterrence and rehabilitation (restoring a prisoner to normal life after their sentence has been served), while removing dangerous people from society.

Abolition gathers pace

The movement towards complete abolition gathered speed in the second half of the twentieth century. In many countries, anti-death penalty campaigners lobbied politicians and held demonstrations outside prisons before and during executions. The abolition movement found support in human rights organizations, including the International Commission of Jurists and Amnesty International. International organizations, including the United Nations (UN) and the Council of

▼ The twentieth century saw an increase in protests against the death penalty. Here, in London in 1935, police question the occupants of a van belonging to campaigners demanding abolition. The protesters are on their way to a demonstration outside Wandsworth Prison, where an execution is about to take place.

▲ In 2006, in Dhaka, Bangladesh, a young member of the Rakhaing Women's Union protests against human rights abuses, including state-sponsored killing, in Myanmar. The Rakhaing people are an ethnic minority group living in Myanmar.

Europe, developed human rights standards restricting or abolishing the death penalty. As a result, an increasing number of countries abolished the death penalty for all crimes.

This table shows the number of countries that have abolished the death penalty for all crimes since 1900.

Year	Number of countries
1900	3
1948	8
1978	19
1998	62
2005	86

Source: Amnesty International

summary

▶ The death penalty is the most extreme form of punishment a government can use on its citizens.

▶ 122 countries no longer use the death penalty.

▶ 74 countries retain and use the death penalty.

▶ 4 countries – China, Iran, Saudi Arabia and the USA – account for 94 per cent of all known executions.

weblinks

For more information about organizations working to abolish the death penalty internationally go to www.waylinks.co.uk/Ethical Debates/deathpenalty

CHAPTER 2

Is the death penalty ever justified?

The death penalty is an important issue in religious and ethical debates because it raises questions about life and death, good and evil, individual choice and public good. The debate about whether the death penalty is right or wrong has been continuing for centuries.

Some religious groups, such as Quakers or Jains, hold that all life is sacred and that no one has the right to take a life. They believe that life is given by God and only God can take it away. Others support a limited use of the death penalty in certain circumstances, while some see it as an essential part of a moral or religious framework.

Some groups quote passages from the Bible or the Koran to support their views. However, they are very selective about the quotes they choose and often use them out of context. Christians have spoken out both for and against capital punishment. As a rule, the Old Testament is used to support punishment and retribution ('an eye for an eye, a tooth for a tooth'), and the New Testament is quoted in favour of

It's a fact

On 1 March 2005, the US Supreme Court ruled by five votes to four that the use of the death penalty against people under the age of 18 at the time of the offence conflicts with the US Constitutional ban on 'cruel and unusual punishments'.

▼ Worshippers honour a Jain saint in India. Jains believe all life is sacred and that all souls are equal. It is against their faith to kill any person, no matter what crime he or she may have committed.

▲ A living death: convicts are packed on to barges for their transportation from Algeria to French Guiana around 1900.

love and forgiveness ('turning the other cheek'). The Koran is sometimes used to justify severe punishments, including the death penalty (under Sharia – Islamic – law), yet many Muslims do not believe in such punishments or want to live under such harsh laws.

Human rights

In a more secular and diverse society, many people look to a wider range of sources for guidance. They rely on family and friends, teachers and classmates, politics, the law and the media to shape their ethical views. Although religious leaders continue to play a prominent role on both sides of the death penalty debate, it is mainly discussed as a human rights issue and in relation to the responsibilities that governments have towards their people and people have towards one another. These rights and responsibilities are embodied in national constitutions and legal systems, and in international law.

The most basic human right is an individual's right to live in safety and security. However, interpretations vary as to how this right relates to the death penalty. Supporters of the death penalty say that governments must retain the right to execute those who kill others and threaten safety and security. Opponents say that governments should not use the death penalty to deprive a person of their life – even if he or she has killed others.

Applying the penalty

If the death penalty is acceptable, when should it be used? In the past, it has sometimes been used very widely. In eighteenth-century England, over 200 crimes were punishable by death – including the theft of a sheep, a spoon or a handkerchief. Not all those sentenced were executed. Some were branded with a hot iron, or transported to America or Australia. Then again, many of those who were transported saw it as a living death.

▲ Public hangings were common in eighteenth-century England, where the death penalty could be imposed for minor offences.

In some countries where the Church played a dominant role, the death penalty was routinely used for sexual offences (rape, adultery, homosexuality) and religious offences (blasphemy, converting to another religion, or converting others). Today, some Muslim countries practising Sharia law use the death penalty in a similar way.

Most countries that retain the death penalty use it only for the most severe crimes, usually pre-meditated murder, treason and terrorist acts. Exceptions include China where, in addition to murder, the death penalty is used for other violent crimes and for non-violent crimes including tax fraud, embezzlement and drug offences, and Singapore, where it is used for drug-related crimes (see page 37). In 1999, the United Nations Commission on Human Rights urged governments which retained the death penalty to use it only for 'intentional crimes with lethal or extremely grave consequences' and not for 'non-violent financial crimes or for non-violent religious practice or expression of conscience'.

Supporters of the death penalty argue that restricting its use to the most serious crimes has given it greater credibility. They say this demonstrates that it is being used as an instrument of justice, rather than for retribution or revenge. Many opponents of the death penalty have also supported restrictions, both for practical reasons (it saves people who would otherwise die) and as a step to total abolition.

Who should receive the death penalty?

Should some people be exempt from the death penalty altogether? Human rights standards say that the following groups should not be subject to the death penalty: children and young people under 18 years of age at the time of the crime; and people who do not understand or cannot be held responsible for their actions, for example, those with mental illness or mental retardation (severe learning difficulties).

The United Nations Convention on the Rights of the Child, signed by all countries except the USA and Somalia, forbids capital punishment for children. However, some executions still take place (see the case study on page 17). In 2005, the US Supreme Court ruled that no person under the age of 18 at the time of the crime should be subject to the death penalty.

Punishing the worst crimes

Opponents of the death penalty argue that even the worst crimes should not be punishable by death. However, many people argue that there are some crimes so terrible that death is the only just punishment. These include pre-meditated murder, torture and mutilation, and 'crimes against humanity'. Such crimes involve deliberate and calculated mass killings, mainly during wars, foreign occupations and uprisings.

◀ In 2005, two suspected Malaysian drug traffickers sit in front of a haul of amphetamines – a type of Class A drug – at the narcotics control board in Bangkok. Both the Malaysian and Thai governments maintain that strict anti-drug laws and the death penalty have helped to combat the drug problem in their country.

Mr. Chia Yok Kong

Mr. Hew Kien Fa

viewpoints

'Simply put, there is a class of people whose crimes are so heinous [evil] ... that the death penalty should apply.'
Paul Rosenweig, Heritage Foundation, 2003

'Children are just a completely different class from adults, and they need to be protected.'
Sue Gunawardena-Vaughn, Amnesty International USA

Surely the perpetrators of mass death deserve the death penalty? At the Nuremberg Trials of 1945-9, dozens of Nazi leaders found guilty of war crimes were sentenced to death and executed. The court considered that this was the only right and just way to punish such evil. Today the argument has shifted against the death penalty in such cases. The International War Crimes Tribunals established to try those responsible for war crimes in former Yugoslavia and Rwanda cannot impose the death penalty – the maximum sentence they can impose is life imprisonment.

Supporters of the death penalty argue that

this is wrong. Their arguments are straightforward. People who commit the worst crimes should themselves be subject to death – the ultimate penalty. By allowing such people to live, we are dishonouring the victims, denying justice to the survivors and making a mockery of the court's purpose.

Opponents say that the death penalty demeans the court and places lawgivers in the same moral position as the lawless. They argue that executions perpetuate revenge and lead to further violence, instead of supporting truth and reconciliation. On a practical level, they point to the fact that few leaders actually

▼ In 1994 in Rwanda military commanders ordered the mass killing of civilians. Almost one million people were killed. This picture shows a survivor of the Rwandan genocide looking at photographs of the victims. Should the perpetrators of genocide receive the death penalty?

stand trial, some are already dead by the time of trial, and others escape. Instead, the less important criminals are the ones who are brought to trial.

▲ Slobodan Milosevic (right), the former leader of Yugoslavia, was put on trial for crimes against humanity. He appeared before the International Criminal Tribunal at the Hague in the Netherlands in 2001.

summary

▶ Supporters believe that governments can protect people by retaining the death penalty for murder and serious crimes.

▶ Opponents believe that governments should not take life, whatever the circumstances.

▶ International human rights law forbids the execution of people who are under 18 years of age at the time of their crime.

case study

Gao Pan

Gao Pan came from a small village in China's Hebei Province. In May 2002, he was convicted of murdering a neighbour during an attempted robbery. Gao Pan was given the death sentence. In April 2003, Gao Pan's lawyer appealed on the grounds that his client was less than 18 years of age when he committed the crime. In 1997, China had outlawed the death sentence for prisoners who were 16 or 17 years of age when the crime was committed. Nevertheless, courts do not always take sufficient care to determine the real age.

This was the case with Gao Pan. Gao's lawyer produced 32 items of evidence supporting the claim that Gao had been under 18 when he committed the murder. The court claimed he was over 18, as recorded in his household registration document, but experts said that the document signature had been falsified (altered). However, Gao's elementary school certificate said that he had been born in August 1984. Gao's family wanted to pay for a test to verify his age by examining a sample of his bone tissue, but the court refused.

Gao Pan's appeal was rejected. His lawyer tried to petition the Supreme People's Court and the National People's Congress. However, on 8 March 2004, while his lawyer was in Beijing, Gao was executed.

weblinks

For more information about the death penalty in China go to www.waylinks.co.uk/Ethical Debates/deathpenalty

CHAPTER 3

Death – the final reckoning

The death penalty is different from any other punishment in one significant respect – it is absolutely final. Once a person has been executed there is no way back. For supporters of the death penalty this is one of its main strengths. It is the ultimate punishment, reserved for the worst offenders, and it removes them permanently from society.

But the death penalty means that there is no room for error or ambiguity. What if the executed person later turns out to be innocent, or new circumstances cast doubt on his or her guilt? This is one of the most powerful arguments put forward by the opponents of the death penalty.

Executing an innocent person

Miscarriages of justice have fuelled the abolitionist movement. For example, in 1950, Timothy Evans was hanged in London for the murder of his baby daughter. Evans had already made – and retracted – several confessions of guilt. He had learning difficulties and confessed easily under police pressure. It later emerged that the murderer was almost certainly Evans' neighbour, John Christie, who had given evidence against him at his trial. Although Timothy Evans was executed, he was granted a posthumous free pardon in 1966. This miscarriage of justice contributed to the abolition of capital punishment in the UK in 1965.

▲ Crowds gather in London to watch the arrest of John Reginald Christie for the murder of his wife in 1953. Timothy Evans had been hanged for another murder, almost certainly committed by Christie, in 1950.

It's a fact

On 15 April 2006, President Gloria Macapagal Arroyo of the Philippines commuted all death sentences to life imprisonment. This is thought to be the world's largest ever commutation of death sentences, which will lead to the reprieve of at least 1,230 people.

There are many reasons for miscarriages of justice. Confused or distressed people like Timothy Evans may make false confessions, have confessions forced from them by police or even have evidence planted against them. They may not understand what is happening to them, especially if they are young, uneducated, or have a mental illness or learning difficulties. They may have an incompetent or inexperienced lawyer who advises them to plead guilty in the hope of getting a lesser sentence. They may face a judge who conducts the trial badly or a jury that does not understand the evidence, or is prejudiced against them. None of these things should happen in a good justice system, but they sometimes do – especially when the defendant is poor and does not have access to a good lawyer.

Release from death row

In the USA there have been many instances where it has been alleged that innocent people have been executed – especially those with poor legal representation. Between 1963 and 2006, more than 120 prisoners were exonerated and had their death sentences commuted. Some had their convictions overturned, and were re-tried and acquitted, or pardoned by the governor. But the appeals process is not easy and can take on average, 9.2 years.

These cases took a new twist in the 1990s with the development of sophisticated forensic testing, using DNA evidence. New independent tests can be applied to previously collected and tested police evidence to determine guilt or innocence. Unfortunately in many cases DNA evidence has been lost, destroyed or not collected.

The most dramatic impact has been seen in the US state of Illinois where, between 1977 and 2000, 13 death row prisoners were found to have been not guilty. The Republican governor of Illinois, George Ryan, was deeply troubled by this and declared a moratorium on executions in January 2003. Governor Ryan was (and remains) a supporter of capital punishment, but he stated that he could no longer support a system that executed innocent people.

Governor Ryan of Illinois, right, ▶ was troubled by the number of death row prisoners who proved to be innocent. Before he left office in 2003, he commuted 164 death sentences to life without parole.

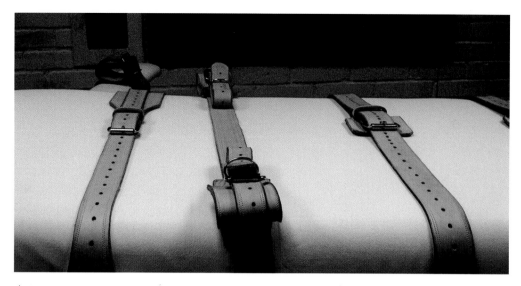

▲ The lethal injection execution table in a Texas prison. At the time of execution, prisoners are strapped to a gurney (a wheeled stretcher) before being given the injection.

The price of justice

The argument that innocent people may be wrongly executed is a strong one and has influenced public opinion against the death penalty. But supporters of the death penalty are able to marshal a range of arguments to support their case too. First, they say that the vast majority of those executed are guilty and that many pleas of innocence are false – deliberate ploys to prolong the appeal process and delay execution. Some supporters declare that there have been no cases in which death row prisoners in the USA have actually been proved innocent – all that has happened is that some doubt has been cast on their *degree* of guilt.

Some supporters go much further. They agree that a tiny number of innocent people may have been executed, but say that this is a small price to pay for the benefit of removing many guilty people permanently from society. They say that there will always be some mistakes, and we just have to accept that this is the price of justice. Some supporters point out that we apply impossibly high standards to the legal system, while we do not expect such standards in other areas of life. For example, thousands of innocent people die in traffic accidents, but very few people argue that we should ban cars.

Other supporters admit that the present system is flawed but that it should be reformed – 'mended, not ended'. They reject a complete review of every case because this would be lengthy and very costly. They point out that the system already allows for a long and elaborate appeals process, which should point out any errors. In any case, modern forensic techniques, including DNA analysis, mean that

It's a fact

The numbers of prisoners on death row worldwide are estimated to be between 19,500 and 24,500.

errors become less frequent, making convictions much safer.

Supporters also say that the finality of the death penalty should encourage prisoners to reveal the truth, since they have nothing to lose by doing so. Opponents of the death penalty argue that keeping prisoners alive gives them the chance to make amends and confess their crime, even years after the trial. It can help to uncover the truth about what happened and this, in the end, may help the victims' families come to terms with their loss. Prisoners may use their lives to repent and do good. For example, former gang leader and convicted murderer, Stanley 'Tookie' Williams, used his years in prison on death row to speak out against gangland warfare. But, despite an international campaign to save his life, he was executed in December 2005.

viewpoints

'I couldn't care less. I've come to the conclusion that the death penalty is a necessary evil.'
Kenneth Stolle, state senator for West Virginia, March 2000

'I now favor a moratorium because I have grave concerns about our state's shameful record of convicting innocent people and putting them on death row. I can't support a system which, in its administration, has proven to be so fraught with error and has come so close to the ultimate nightmare, the state's taking of innocent life.'
Governor George Ryan of Illinois, May 2001

▼ Stanley 'Tookie' Williams, a former gang leader on death row, wrote a series of books urging young people not to get involved with gangs, drugs and crime.

Making martyrs

Opponents of the death penalty argue that execution may glorify prisoners and make them martyrs in the eyes of their supporters. This is especially true of prisoners who espouse a political cause. In 1916, the British government executed 15 Irish nationalists who had led a brief but violent uprising against British rule in Ireland. The nationalists wanted Ireland to be politically independent from Britain.

Their executions were intended to quash the rebellion, but instead they increased popular support for Irish nationalism and ultimately led to Irish independence. The executed men are now remembered by many as martyrs and heroes.

Zacarias Moussaoui wanted to be a martyr. The US government alleged that he had actively plotted to carry out attacks on the World Trade Center in New York and the

▼ This photograph of the bombed Pentagon building on fire on 11 September 2001 was introduced as evidence at the trial of Zacarias Moussaoui in April 2006.

weblinks

For more information about US anti-death penalty campaigns go to www.waylinks.co.uk/Ethical Debates/deathpenalty

Pentagon in Washington DC on 11 September 2001. He was charged with conspiracy to commit acts of terrorism and murder. The jury had the power to hand down a death sentence. After a long trial, in May 2006 the jury decided against the death sentence on the grounds that Moussaoui had played only a limited role in the planned attacks. Nine jurors also said that Moussaoui had been affected by an unstable and abusive childhood. Moussaoui was sentenced to life imprisonment without parole in a maximum-security prison.

It's a fact

In China, Teng Xingshan was convicted of the murder of a waitress in 1987 and, despite his pleas of innocence, was executed in 1989. Years later, Teng's children tracked down the waitress living in her home town. Teng was posthumously exonerated in January 2006.

summary

▶ Unlike other punishments, the death penalty is final and cannot be reversed.

▶ Opponents say that miscarriages of justice result in innocent people being executed or sent to death row – in recent US cases innocence has been proved through the use of DNA testing.

▶ Supporters say that few innocent people are executed and DNA testing will make convictions safer.

case study

Ryan Matthews

Ryan Matthews was 17 when he was arrested and charged with the murder of a local shopkeeper in Bridge City, Louisiana, USA, in April 1997. The murderer had worn a ski mask and was described by three witnesses as 'short'. Ryan Matthews was six feet tall, and there was no DNA evidence on the ski mask to link Ryan to the murder.

Poor, black and with learning difficulties, Ryan already faced huge barriers. But there were even more at his trial in May 1999. His court-appointed lawyer was unprepared, failed to investigate the facts, and did not understand the DNA evidence. Eleven of the twelve jurors were white, in an area where one-third of the population was black. The trial took only three days – on the second day the judge insisted that the jury stay late into the night to make a decision. Ryan was declared guilty, and two days later was given a death sentence.

Campaigners took up Ryan's case, and new lawyers investigated new leads. They found that the DNA in the ski mask matched the profile of another man already in prison for murder. This man had been boasting that he had committed the crime for which Ryan had been convicted.

In April 2004, a new trial was arranged based on the new evidence, and findings that the prosecution had suppressed evidence. A few months later, the prosecutor dropped all the charges against Ryan and he was free to rebuild his shattered life. Ryan Matthews was the fourteenth death row inmate to be exonerated with the help of DNA testing.

CHAPTER 4

Can the death penalty ever be humane?

Execution by fire, stoning, beheading, hanging, slow and prolonged torture – all these methods have been used to inflict the death penalty. Some of them are still used today. The government of Saudi Arabia beheads people, and hangings and stonings have been used in Iran. In both countries the punishments have been carried out in front of crowds in public places. Well into the 1990s in China, criminals were shot after they had been paraded through the streets with placards declaring their crimes hanging around their necks.

Some supporters of the death penalty argue that painful and public executions are necessary to ensure that justice is not only done, but seen to be done. They say that the pain, distress and indignity inflicted are part of the punishment and act as a vivid deterrent to would-be criminals. But opponents argue that such executions are degrading. The condemned people are denied dignity and privacy in their last moments, and the watching crowds are whipped into a bloodthirsty frenzy. Opponents say that the death penalty is a 'cruel and unusual punishment' and, therefore, a violation of human rights law.

▼ During the French Revolution in the late eighteenth century there were numerous public executions by beheading, using the newly invented guillotine.

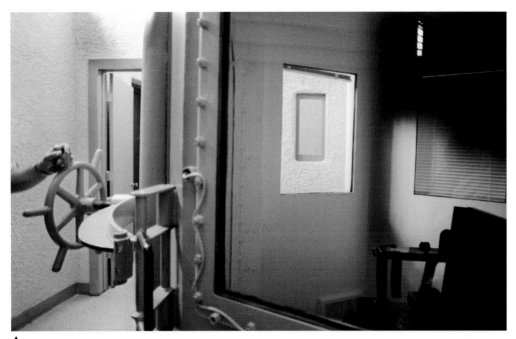

▲ The gas chamber, used widely in the USA during the twentieth century, was considered a quick and relatively painless way to die.

Humane executions?

The trend has been to make the death penalty more 'humane' and to hide it from public sight. The infamous guillotine, first used in 1792 during the French Revolution, was promoted as a quicker, more humane and scientific method of execution. It was used in France until 1977, with the last public execution taking place in 1939. In the UK, public executions ended in 1868. From that time onwards, prisoners were hanged behind prison walls. Some countries used firing squads, which were believed to inflict a quick and relatively painless death.

However, it was in the USA that the greatest efforts were made to make executions 'humane', 'painless' and 'scientific'. New York state first used the electric chair in 1890, killing prisoners

It's a fact

According to the 8th Amendment of the US Constitution, Article 5 of the Universal Declaration of Human Rights, and the European Declaration of Human Rights, the death penalty is a 'cruel and unusual [random] punishment'.

with massive surges of electricity. In 1924, the state of Nevada became the first to use cyanide in a sealed gas chamber. In 1977, the state of Oklahoma started to use lethal injection. In fact, this is made up of three separate injections – the first makes the prisoner unconscious, the second stops muscle movement and the third stops heart beating. Today, lethal injection is by far the most common method of execution in the USA.

▲ New York state first used the electric chair in 1890, killing prisoners with massive surges of electricity. The electric chair remained in use throughout the twentieth century.

Supporters of capital punishment argue that these developments have made the death penalty less painful for the prisoner and more acceptable to the public. Opponents say that, although some methods are more painful than others, none are 'humane'. However 'scientific' the method, executions can go wrong – electricity burns the victim, gas slowly suffocates, lethal injections fail. And it is not just the moment of death that is horrific, but the whole process leading up to it – the mental torture, the dashed hopes for a last-minute reprieve – and, in the USA, the years spent on death row while the legal process grinds on.

Who is responsible?

Making executions 'humane' has meant redefining the role of the executioner.

What person would choose to wield the axe, pull the lever or press the button that leads to death? Supporters say that, when an execution is carried out by a machine operated by teams of people, responsibility is transferred from an individual executioner and becomes a technical matter.

In practice, however, is this really the case? Opponents argue that machinery is never neutral – it still has to be built, maintained and operated by individuals. For example, in May 2006 Amnesty International drew attention to the activities of an English man who claimed he built gallows and hanging equipment for export to the Middle East and Africa. In August 2006 this practice was banned under new regulations which prohibit European Union countries from exporting torture equipment.

A painful death

Opponents argue that death by machine may be more painful than when it was in the hands of a responsible individual. Consider death by lethal injection as used in the USA. The code of the American Medical Association forbids doctors from delivering lethal injections, although they are allowed to act as witnesses and confirm that death has occurred. The result is that technicians, prison guards or orderlies take on the tasks of finding a suitable vein on the condemned person's body and attaching the injection line. Sometimes this is done poorly, resulting in prolonged suffering and painful death. For example, in Ohio in May 2006, Joseph L. Clark took 90 minutes to die, after two botched attempts to find a suitable vein.

Supporters say that executions can be carried out carefully and professionally, with proper safeguards against cruel executioners or methods. Opponents say that everyone associated with the death penalty, even in a supporting role, is tainted by the process.

Until recently, David Lucas, an English farmer and carpenter, was building gallows and hanging equipment for export. The practice is now banned in the UK.

v i e w p o i n t s

'As harsh as it sounds, if lethal injection is good enough to end the suffering of a beloved pet, it is probably too good for a pre-meditated murderer.'
Ronald Bailey, *Reason* magazine (an online political journal for 'free minds and free markets'), April 2006

'Obviously this man was suffering. This was a violent death – an ugly event. We put animals to death more humanely.'
Cameron Harper, television journalist, after witnessing the death of Donald Eugene Harding in the gas chamber, Arizona, USA, 1992

▲ In Manila, in the Philippines, inmates share a cell at a jail. Long imprisonment, perhaps for life, is an alternative to the death penalty.

Alternative punishments

What are the alternatives to capital punishment? Since the death penalty is most commonly used to punish the crime of murder, what other methods could be used to deliver justice for this offence? In earlier times, punishments included mutilation, compensation to the victim's family ('blood money'), and voluntary or involuntary exile, but none of these options would be feasible or acceptable to modern society.

The most common alternative is life imprisonment, either for a fixed time (usually between ten and twenty years) after which the prisoner might be released, or life without parole, which means the prisoner will never be released. Some supporters argue that life imprisonment can never be an adequate punishment for taking life – all murderers should receive the death penalty. More commonly, supporters accept that life imprisonment is appropriate in some cases, but argue that the death sentence should be retained for the very worst crimes – such as pre-meditated killings, serial killings, murders of children, or aggravated offences where murder is combined with rape or torture.

Opponents point out that the death penalty is not awarded to the worst offenders but to the poorest and most vulnerable – especially to those who cannot afford a good lawyer, independent DNA testing, or a thorough investigation of the facts. Furthermore, because of long waits on death row, often ten years or more, those receiving a death sentence are in effect serving both a life and death sentence. Opponents believe that a life sentence, even one without parole, can give the prisoner hope and an opportunity to repent and reform.

summary

▶ Over the past century, the trend has been to make executions more 'humane'.

▶ Opponents say that the death penalty is never humane but always cruel and painful.

▶ Supporters say that executions can be carried out carefully and professionally.

▶ The most common alternative punishment is life imprisonment, with or without parole.

It's a fact

Since 1990, eight countries are known to have executed prisoners who were under 18 years old at the time of the crime – China, Democratic Republic of Congo, Iran, Nigeria, Pakistan, Saudi Arabia, the USA and Yemen. In 2005, eight children under 18 years of age were executed in Iran.

case study

Albert Pierrepont

Albert Pierrepont (1905-92) served as chief hangman of the United Kingdom for many years, following his father and uncle who had also been hangmen. The job of a hangman was not full-time, however; Pierrepont was also a delivery driver and, later, a pub landlord. Pierrepont took great pride in ensuring that his executions were as quick and humane as possible, and that his prisoners were treated with dignity both before and after death.

Pierrepont became the most prolific hangman in British history. In his later years he became well known and faced the wrath of demonstrators against capital punishment. Altogether, he executed 433 people, including almost 200 Nazi war criminals. Of the others, most were convicted murderers – although some were later proved to have been innocent.

In his autobiography, Pierrepont turned against the death penalty, saying: 'I have come to the conclusion that executions solve nothing, and are only an antiquated relic of a primitive desire for revenge which takes the easy way and hands over the responsibility for revenge to other people.... The trouble with the death penalty has always been that nobody wanted it for everybody, but everybody differed about who should get off.'

CHAPTER 5

Who dies and who lives?

Can the death penalty ever be applied fairly? This is one of the most contentious issues in the death penalty debate.

The meaning of fairness

Fairness means there should not be discrimination on racial, ethnic, religious, political or other grounds, and people should receive equal treatment before the law regardless of whether they are rich or poor. No one should be put on trial unless there is a genuine case to answer, and evidence must be properly collected; witnesses, police and the legal system should not be incompetent or corrupt. All prisoners must have proper legal counsel and receive a fair trial. Trials should not be rushed, all the evidence must be heard in court, and juries should not be biased. Special circumstances need to be taken into account, including mental illness, learning difficulties and domestic violence. A proper appeals process needs to be in place so that errors and omissions can be corrected.

▼ A hidden photographer captures the beheading of an alleged drug dealer in Jeddah, Saudi Arabia. Many executions take place after secretive or unfair trials.

Does discrimination exist?

The secrecy that often surrounds the death penalty means that it is hard to know the extent of discrimination. In many countries, trials are blatantly unfair and prisoners are sentenced and executed with great haste. In some countries, certain groups may be unfairly treated. For example, in Saudi Arabia, migrant workers with few rights are more likely to be executed than Saudi citizens.

The most detailed evidence comes from the USA. Opponents of the death penalty point out that the overwhelming majority of people who are sentenced to death are poor and badly educated. Many belong to ethnic, racial or other minorities, and some are mentally ill or disabled. These groups are more likely to undergo trials that are unfair or incomplete, with biased juries, and they are less likely to have a good legal team or to understand the court system. Therefore, opponents conclude that the death penalty is unfair, arbitrary and racially discriminatory.

Supporters of the death penalty answer these charges in two ways. Some deny any bias in the system; others agree there is bias, but argue that this is a reflection of society as a whole rather than a problem with the legal system.

How racial discrimination works

Racial bias is a major area of debate. African-Americans (blacks) are more likely to be imprisoned than other groups. While African-Americans make up only 12 per cent of the US population, they represent almost 50 per cent of convicted prisoners. Of the 3,700 prisoners on death row, 42 per cent are black, 45 per cent are white and 10.5 are Hispanic (Latin-American). Over one-third of those executed since 1976 have been African-Americans (see table A below).

On average, blacks are poorer than whites, more likely to live in bad housing in violent neighbourhoods, and less likely to finish school or attend college. So it could be argued that it is understandable that more African-Americans are tried, jailed and executed for violent crimes as their lives tend to be more difficult.

However, the evidence of discrimination is more precise. Research shows that the race of the victim is the single most important factor in determining who is given the death penalty. The death sentence is most often given when blacks kill whites, but only rarely given when whites kill blacks. Between 1976 and 2006, 80 per cent of those executed were convicted of killing white people, compared with only 14 per cent who were convicted of killing blacks (see table B).

Table A shows the racial background of prisoners executed in the USA (1976-July 2006)

Racial background of executed prisoners	Racial background of executed prisoners in numbers	Racial background of executed prisoners as percentage of total
Black	351	34
White	588	58
Hispanic	68	6
Other	24	2
Total	1,031	100

Source: The Death Penalty Information Center website

Table B shows the racial background of murder victims of prisoners executed in the USA (1976-May 2006)

Racial background of murder victims	Racial background of murder victims in numbers	Racial background of murder victims in percentages
Black	215	14
White	1,224	80
Hispanic	72	4
Other	32	2

Source: The Death Penalty Information Center website

▲ African-Americans and other minorities are more likely to receive the death penalty than white people. Here in Los Angeles, USA, protesters gather and pray as the convicted ex-street gang member Stanley 'Tookie' Williams is executed.

It's a fact

In Texas, between 1976 and 2006, not a single white person was executed for killing a black person.

Jury bias

Another issue for concern is how juries are composed. Under US law, some jurors can be rejected because they hold prejudiced views or attitudes that would affect their judgement. Although the race of the juror is not supposed to be taken into account, it has been a common practice for black jurors to be excluded from cases where the prisoner is black, even in areas where blacks are a majority, or large minority, of the population. Research shows that jury prejudice or indifference can affect the outcome of a case. This is especially important in states where juries, rather than judges, determine the sentence, including the death sentence.

In 1987, an assistant attorney in Pennsylvania even stated in a training video: 'The only way you're going to do your best is to get jurors that are unfair, and more likely to convict than anybody else in that room.... And it may appear as if you're being racist, but again, you're just being realistic.' When the videotape came to light ten years later, it gave new grounds for appeal in a number of death penalty cases.

Discrimination, or not?

Supporters of the death penalty have answered concerns about racial discrimination in different ways. Some are frankly racist and support a discriminatory system. Others deny discrimination, saying that the research is wrong or the statistics are wrongly interpreted. A more considered view admits that the system works against minorities and poor and vulnerable prisoners, but that this reflects the racial discrimination and economic divisions present in US society. These supporters argue that the legal system itself is sound and that any flaws can be corrected through the appeals system.

summary

▶ All trials and punishments, including the death penalty, should be based on the principles of fairness and non-discrimination.

▶ Opponents say that the death penalty is given in a biased and discriminatory way, and is more likely to be given to poor people, ethnic minorities and people without proper legal counsel. US research supports this view.

▶ Supporters say that the death penalty is not discriminatory and reflects inequalities in the wider society.

case study

Anthony Green

In November 1987, Anthony Green robbed, shot and killed Susan Babich in a shopping mall. He was quickly arrested and soon admitted his guilt. In many ways, 22-year-old Anthony was an unlikely killer. He had done well in school and had no previous convictions. However, he did have a drug problem.

In other states Anthony might have received a long jail sentence. However, he was a black man living in Charleston County, South Carolina, and Susan was a white woman. The state had a record of racial bias – a black person killing a white person was 3.5 times more likely to be sentenced to death than a white killing a black, and Charleston County had the worst record of all. Here, a black person was 14 times more likely to be sentenced to death than a white person.

Anthony spent 15 years on death row. His lawyers appealed repeatedly to the state and federal courts, arguing that the death penalty arose from racial bias. All the appeals failed. The Inter-American Court of Human Rights, of which the USA is a member, asked South Carolina to postpone the execution until it could determine whether or not the case was racially biased. Despite their appeal, Anthony Green was executed by lethal injection in August 2002.

weblinks

For more information about the death penalty in the USA go to www.waylinks.co.uk/Ethical Debates/deathpenalty

CHAPTER 6

Does the death penalty make society safer?

Supporters of capital punishment argue that the death penalty makes society safer in two ways – prevention and deterrence.

Prevention

One of the most straightforward arguments in favour of the death penalty is that it removes dangerous criminals permanently from society. Put crudely, it states that: 'every murderer put to death is one less that is going to kill you.'

Opponents say that life imprisonment has the same outcome, without resorting to the death penalty. In any case, they point out that the number of people executed is very small in relation to the number of criminals. For example, in 2004 there were 16,137 murders in the USA but only 59 executions. Supporters say that this means the death penalty should be used more frequently, and that even when it is used sparingly it still acts as a deterrent.

Deterrence

One of the most common arguments in favour of the death penalty is that it acts as a deterrent – people are less likely to commit similar crimes if they know that they will be executed if they do. On the surface, it seems logical that the death penalty would act as a deterrent. Surely the harsher the punishment, the less of a risk a criminal will be prepared to take? Supporters say that deterrence does work and they use complex statistical studies to bolster their argument, typically attempting to prove the number of lives saved by each death sentence. For example, a study from 1975 calculated that one execution prevents seven further murders, another from 2005 said that one execution prevents eighteen murders.

Opponents believe that these figures are wrong, or highly exaggerated, and that the arguments for deterrence are flawed. They say that the motives behind many murders

The relative of a victim of terrorism (right) speaks out ▶ at a conference held by the All India Anti-Terrorist Front (AIATF) in New Delhi in 2005. The AIATF raises awareness of terrorist violence in India and lobbies government to uphold the death penalty.

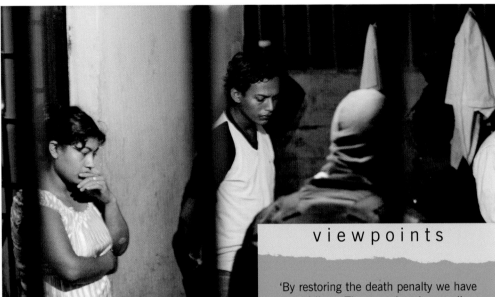

▲ An alleged member and murder suspect of the Mara Salvatrucha gang in El Salvador is arrested. Can the death penalty act as a deterrent within violent gang societies?

are not rational; murders are often committed by people who are mentally disturbed or under the influence of drink or drugs. If a person lives in a violent environment, where the threat of death is ever present, perhaps through a drive-by shooting or a revenge attack, then he or she will be hardened to violence. The death penalty, therefore, might seem less threatening than it would to other people.

Opponents also say that any deterrent effect is relatively short-term and its impact soon fades. Supporters say that the solution is to decrease the time between sentencing and execution and to give greater publicity when the death sentence is carried out. They state that these measures would ensure that the impact remains, long after the execution.

viewpoints

'By restoring the death penalty we have saved lives. There are loved ones alive today because we were strong enough to be tough enough to do what was necessary to protect innocent people. Preventing a crime from being committed ultimately is more important than punishing criminals after they have shattered innocent lives.'
George E. Pataki, governor of New York state, 1997

'The penalty exacts a terrible price in dollars, lives, and human decency. Rather than tamping down the flames of violence, it fuels them.... I urge all of our lawmakers, in the strongest possible terms, not to reinstate the death penalty in New York.'
Robert M. Morgenthau, district attorney, Manhattan, New York, 2004

It's a fact

Since 1973, 123 prisoners have been released in the USA after evidence emerged of their innocence of the crimes for which they were sentenced to death.

Measuring deterrence

In reality, it is almost impossible to measure the deterrent effect, because it means trying to relate causes and effects, which are complex and often not measurable. One way is to look at societies that have abolished the death penalty to see if they are more violent than societies that have kept it.

The table below left shows that murder rates in European countries where the death penalty has been abolished are lower than rates in the USA. Does this mean that, rather than having a deterrent effect, the death penalty encourages violent crime? We simply do not know because so many other factors come into play. For example, the USA has a much higher rate of gun ownership – and gun murders – than Europe. And how do we explain the fact that Japan, which retains the death penalty, has the lowest murder rate of all?

Similarly the table below right shows that US states which retain the death penalty generally have higher murder rates than those that do not. Opponents could argue this shows that the death penalty is no deterrent to murder, while supporters could argue that higher crime rates need more severe punishments. Neither argument explains why murder rates are falling across the USA, both in death penalty and non-death penalty states, while the number of executions is also falling. The explanation seems to lie in a combination of factors, including long-term changes in society, and more and better policing.

---

weblinks

For more information about pro-death penalty views in the USA go to www.waylinks.co.uk/EthicalDebates/deathpenalty

---

This table shows murders per capita 1998-2000 – selected countries

Country	Death penalty	Murders per 100,000 people
Jamaica	YES	32.40
Mexico	NO	13.60
USA	YES	4.28
France	NO	1.73
Australia	NO	1.50
Canada	NO	1.49
United Kingdom	NO	1.40
Germany	NO	1.16
New Zealand	NO	1.11
Denmark	NO	1.06
Ireland	NO	0.92
Japan	YES	0.49

Source: Seventh United Nations Survey of Crime Trends and Operations of Criminal Justice System 1998-2000

This table shows murders per capita 2004 – selected US states

State	Death penalty	Murders per 100,000 people
Mississippi	YES	7.8
Michigan	NO	6.4
Texas	YES	6.1
Florida	YES	5.4
Oklahoma	YES	5.3
Virginia	YES	5.2
Wisconsin	NO	2.8
Massachusetts	NO	2.6
Rhode Island	NO	2.4
North Dakota	NO	1.4
US average		5.5

Source: Death Penalty Information Center, using US crime statistics

case study

Nguyen Tuong Van

On 2 December 2005, Nguyen Tuong Van was hanged in Singapore's Changi prison. He had been convicted of smuggling 396 grams of heroin through Singapore airport, en route to Australia. Singapore's Misuse of Drugs Act prescribes the death penalty for any person caught possessing over 15 grams of heroin.

Nguyen was an Australian citizen who had left Vietnam as a child. His plight gained huge attention in Australia, where the death penalty had long been abolished. The Australian government pleaded for mercy. His lawyers argued that his youth (he was 21 when caught), his circumstances (he was attempting to pay off debts owed by his twin brother, a former heroin addict) and the fact that he had confessed immediately should have counted in his favour. On the eve of Nguyen's execution, his lawyer, Lex Lasry, said:

▲ Flowers cover Nguyen Tuong Van's coffin in a Singapore funeral parlour.

'He is not without blame – he accepts that.... He has a very strong insight into the harm heroin does ... he has become, in my view, a beacon for young people who might be tempted to be exploited in this way to overcome the temptation and to transform their lives.'

Abdullah Tarmugi, the speaker of the Parliament of Singapore, defended the use of the death penalty as a deterrent to others. He said: 'Nguyen was caught in possession of almost 400 grams of pure heroin, enough for more than 26,000 doses of heroin for drug addicts.... He knew what he was doing and the consequences of his actions.' However, Chee Soon Juan, leader of the Singapore Democratic Party, argued against the death penalty, saying that it was too harsh on drug couriers such as Nguyen and had little effect on the drug bosses who controlled the trade.

summary

▶ Supporters say that the death penalty permanently removes dangerous criminals from society.

▶ Opponents say that life imprisonment has the same result.

▶ Supporters believe that the death penalty acts as a deterrent – other people are less likely to commit similar crimes if they know they will be executed – and quote statistical studies to support their view.

▶ Opponents say that any deterrent effect will be short-term.

▶ In reality, it is almost impossible to measure the deterrent effect and it is difficult to relate the level of crime to the use of the death penalty.

CHAPTER 7

The death penalty and society

▲ The murder of a young child – like two-year-old
James Bulger in Liverpool – often leads to an
increase in support for the death penalty.

What do people really think about the
death penalty? When the Gallup
Organization conducted an international
opinion poll in 2000, they found a small
majority – 52 per cent – in favour of it. But
this varied considerably by region (see the
table opposite).

It's a fact

On 29 August 2005, just two days before
Arthur Baird was scheduled to be executed,
Indiana governor Mitch Daniels commuted
his death sentence on grounds of
mental illness.

Public opinion

Supporters and opponents of the death penalty interpret these findings to give credibility to their own views. Supporters point out that public support for capital punishment remains high, even in countries where it has long been abolished. Opponents point out that, as more countries abolish or stop using capital punishment, so public opinion changes and support for the death penalty fades.

In general, people tend to support the existing policy of their country. So, in abolitionist countries, support is lower than in those that retain capital punishment. Even so, polls often register quite a high level of support.

In the USA, polls show a majority in favour of the death penalty. However, this support has dropped significantly in the last decade. In 1994, a Gallup poll found 80 per cent in support but this had dropped to 65 per cent by May 2006, with only 47 per cent in support when there was an alternative offered of life imprisonment without parole.

It's a fact

In 2005, India's new chief justice, Justice Y. K. Saberwal, expressed his support for the abolition of the death penalty and said that he would apply it only 'in the rarest of rare cases'.

The questions asked can also influence the answers. For example, a UK poll in the year 2000 recorded clear majorities against the death penalty, except for one category – child murder. In this category, 58 per cent said that the death penalty should apply. Yet in the UK such questions are purely theoretical. Faced with the prospect of a real execution, many people might answer the question rather differently.

Supporters of the death penalty often present it as a quick and cheap process. This is probably true in countries such as China, where execution quickly follows a short trial. It is not true for the USA, where the trial and appeal process take many years. Many prisoners remain on death row for ten or twenty years before they are executed.

This table shows public opinion on the death penalty, according to a Gallup Poll held in the year 2000

Region	For death penalty - %	Against death penalty - %	Don't know/other - %
Africa	54	43	3
America – North	66	27	7
America – South	37	55	8
Asia	63	21	16
Europe – East	60	29	11
Europe – West	34	60	6
Worldwide	52	39	9

Source: Gallup Poll Millennium Polls

The length of time that prisoners spend on death row leads death penalty opponents to say that this is not only inhumane but very expensive, with each death sentence costing an estimated $1.3 million, including legal costs. They say that substituting a life sentence would be better for the prisoner and less costly for society, which could use the money saved to help prevent further crimes. Some supporters argue that changes in the legal system could cut the long appeals process, resulting in quicker executions. Others want to retain the present legal system – they say that it is the principle that is important, not the cost.

Politics and the media

In all of this, however, it is not public opinion that makes the crucial decisions, it is governments. On this issue, governments often act in defiance of public opinion. For example, when members of parliament (MPs) voted to end the death penalty in the UK in 1965, public opinion was in favour of keeping it. Attempts to reintroduce the death penalty in the UK have failed. When the issue came before parliament in 1994 only 159 MPs voted in favour, and 403 voted against. Since then, the UK has signed the sixth protocol of the European Convention of

weblinks▸

For more information about pro-death penalty views in the UK go to www.waylinks.co.uk/Ethical Debates/deathpenalty

▼ A group of Irish men, known as the 'Birmingham Six', spent 16 years in jail after being convicted of terrorist murders. They were later found to be completely innocent and were released in 1991. Had the death penalty been in use in the UK, they would have been executed.

Human Rights, which formally abolished the death penalty for all crimes and ensured that it could not be brought back.

In countries retaining the death penalty, it is often a contentious political issue, with both sides using emotional and sometimes misleading arguments. Politicians try to outdo one another in being tough on crime, sometimes in cynical and underhand ways. For example, in the 1988 US presidential election Senator Michael Dukakis, the Democratic candidate, was asked whether his capital punishment view would change if his wife and children were murdered. When he said 'no', he was branded 'weak' on crime. Presidents Bill Clinton and George W. Bush were pro-death penalty and both signed execution warrants during their times as state governors.

The media can also play an important role on both sides of the issue. It has sometimes supported calls for the death penalty, either in principle or in specific cases, usually those involving particularly terrible murders. Yet the media has also aided anti-death penalty campaigners by highlighting miscarriages of justice.

Victims' families

Although campaigners on both sides feel very strongly about the issue, the fact is that the death penalty plays little or no part in most people's lives. Apart from the condemned prisoners, those who are most affected are their families and the families of the victims. It might be thought that the families of murder victims would be the strongest in support of the death penalty. Yet even here there are many differing views.

It's a fact

Any country applying to join either the European Union or the Council of Europe must agree to abolish the death penalty.

▼ People protesting against the death penalty at a rally in Austin, Texas, in 2000.

A murder victim's family will experience a range of emotions. Their first emotions of grief and distress later turn to anger and despair, and perhaps also to thoughts of revenge and retribution. They must relive these emotions through a police investigation, and later at a trial with all the subsequent publicity. They seek to understand how and why their loved one

died – and very often they are disappointed in what they find. It is not surprising that many want to see the criminal suffer in return, and indeed in many courts victims' families can state their views and wishes in a 'victim impact statement'. In some US states, victims' families may also witness the execution.

For some families, the death penalty is the only proper and just punishment. They feel that by having taken a life, the perpetrator must forfeit his or her own life. Furthermore, it is argued that the death penalty is not simply a matter of justice but is necessary for emotional 'closure'. In other words, only once the criminal has been executed can the family end their suffering and move on with their lives. Supporters of the death penalty often quote the wishes of a victim's family as one of the strongest reasons for its use.

However, opponents of the death penalty feel that this is a dangerous road to follow. They say that punishment should be

weblinks▸

For more information about help for murder victims go to www.waylinks.co.uk/Ethical Debates/deathpenalty

◀ Despite the fact that her own son was killed as a result of gang violence, Vicky D. Lindsey was involved in the campaign to grant clemency to convicted murderer Stanley 'Tookie' Williams (see page 21).

▲ Iranian officials prepare to hang convicted murderer, Hashem Anbarniya, in Tehran on 27 October 2002.

objective and must relate to the circumstances of the crime, not the feelings of the victim. They argue that the death penalty system, with its long-drawn-out procedures, may actually help to heighten feelings of helplessness and frustration, rather than aid closure. Furthermore, they point out that not all victims' families want or support the death penalty. Some oppose it on principle, and others say that it will not relieve their suffering or bring them closure.

A safer society?

Does the use of the death penalty have a wider effect? For example, does it result in a more violent and less compassionate society? Or does it, by providing an ultimate sanction for those who commit the most terrible crimes, make society safer and more law abiding?

Where the death penalty is used widely and indiscriminately, as it was in eighteenth-century England, it is nearly always the sign of a lawless and divided society, where justice is rare and where criminals flourish. No rational person would choose to live in such a society.

Today's supporters of capital punishment argue that it should be retained as an ultimate punishment to be used only in the most serious cases, after full investigation and a fair trial. They say that if the death penalty is used carefully, no law-abiding citizen need fear that his or her life is in danger. Rather, they argue, the death penalty is a sign of how society values life – the life of the vulnerable and the innocent.

Opponents of the death penalty see the situation very differently. They argue that state-sponsored killing has no place in a modern society based on international human rights laws. The death penalty is used overwhelmingly on poor and vulnerable prisoners, including innocent people. Today there are alternative punishments, such as life imprisonment, available for even the most serious crimes. Death penalty opponents see a society without capital punishment as a step towards a less violent and more just world.

case study

Turkey abolishes the death penalty

On 3 August 2002, the Turkish parliament voted to abolish the death penalty in peacetime, as part of a reform to improve human rights. The final parliamentary debate continued for 22 hours, with a majority voting for reforms.

The main motivation was Turkey's desire to join the European Union (EU), which it believed would bring greater prosperity. One condition of EU membership is the abolition of the death penalty.

After the vote, Deputy Premier Mesul Yilmaz said: 'Turkey has taken a giant step on the road to the EU'. The National Action Party voted against abolition, saying that it rewarded terrorists who had fought a 15-year rebellion against the government. The EU said it welcomed the reforms: 'as an important signal of the determination of Turkey's political leaders towards further alignment to the values and standards of the EU.'

The last execution had been in 1984. However, the death penalty remained available and the courts regularly sentenced people to death, mainly for murder and terrorist offences. When the death penalty was abolished, there were 124 inmates on death row, including Kurdish rebel leader Abdullah Ocalan. All will now serve life sentences without the possibility of parole.

weblinks

For more information about anti-death penalty campaigns and legal advice go to www.waylinks.co.uk/Ethical Debates/deathpenalty

viewpoints

'The death penalty is not an initiation of force as is murder; rather it is a response to force – a supremely calculated and necessary one.'
J. Daryl Charles,
Christian Research Journal, 1994

'Capital punishment is an intolerable denial of civil liberties, and is inconsistent with the fundamental values of our democratic system.'
American Civil Liberties Union website, 2006

▲ After five years without the death penalty, Lebanon resumed its use by executing two men by firing squad and one by hanging in January 2004. Here human rights activists protesting against the re-introduction of the death penalty lie down on the main road to the parliament building in Beirut.

Who is winning the argument? More countries are moving towards abolition than ever before. However, even today, most of the world's population still lives in countries where the death penalty remains in use. For now, the question of whether capital punishment should continue to be used is still open to debate.

It's a fact

10 October is the Annual World Day Against the Death Penalty.

summary

▶ In general, people support the existing policy of their country on the death penalty, although support remains high, even in countries that have abolished it. Overall support seems to be falling, including in the USA.

▶ Governments make the decision to retain or abolish the death penalty, but they can react to public opinion or media pressure. However, governments often act in defiance of public opinion.

▶ Countries that join the European Union must agree to abolish the death penalty.

Glossary

Appeal (against a sentence) To apply to a higher court for the reversal of a decision made by a lower court.

Arbitrary Random.

Blasphemy Offensive comments about God or religion.

Clemency The quality of being merciful.

Commute To overturn or turn into something else, for example, a death sentence into life imprisonment.

Constitution A set of laws governing a country or organization.

Deter To discourage or stop.

Deterrence/deterrent An action or law which discourages or prevents something happening.

DNA (deoxyribonucleic acid) A substance present in almost all living organisms as the carrier of genetic information. Every person has his or her own unique DNA.

Enlightenment, the An intellectual movement of the late seventeenth and early eighteenth centuries.

Exonerate To declare a person to be innocent.

Forensic Detailed scientific investigation.

Humane Kind and compassionate.

Indiscriminate Not making a careful choice, arbitrary.

Jains A religious group, originating in western India, with a strong belief in non-violence.

Jurors Members of a jury (usually 12 or 15 people).

Martyr A person who dies, or is prepared to die, for a cause.

Miscarriage of justice The wrongful conviction for a crime.

Moratorium An agreed ban on an activity.

Pardon An official announcement which releases a person from the legal charges against them.

Parole The release of a prisoner, on the promise of good behaviour, before his or her sentence has been fully served.

Penal code A list of punishments for breaking the law.

Perpetrator A person who carries out an act, often an unlawful one.

Perpetuate To cause to continue indefinitely.

Posthumous After death.

Pre-meditate To plan beforehand.

Prosecutor The government-appointed lawyer who takes legal proceedings against a prisoner. In the USA, this is often the district attorney.

Quakers A religious group, also known as the Society of Friends, with a strong foundation in non-violence.

Reconciliation A situation in which people are no longer opposed to one another.

Reprieve To cancel a punishment.

Retract To withdraw, for example, a statement or confession.

Secular Not religious.

Serial killer A person who carries out a series, or string, of killings.

Sharia law The legal system of strict Islamic law, used in some Muslim countries.

Testimony A formal statement given in a court of law.

Treason The crime of betraying one's country.

United Nations An organization founded at the end of the Second World War, with the aim of preventing future wars. Today more than 190 nations belong to the UN.

Timeline

1764 Publication of *On Crimes and Punishments* by Cesare Beccaria, arguing that the death penalty is unjust and does not benefit society.

1786 Grand Duke Leopold abolishes capital punishment in the Duchy of Tuscany.

1890 New York City first uses the electric chair.

1961 New Zealand abolishes the death penalty, last used in 1957, for all crimes except treason. In 1989, the death penalty is abolished for all crimes.

1965 UK abolishes the death penalty for murder in England, Wales and Scotland, initially for five years, but later permanently. Although the death penalty is retained for a small number of crimes, including treason, no further executions take place.

1969 American Convention on Human Rights states that countries retaining the death penalty should only use it for the most serious crimes (and not for political crimes) and that countries that have abolished it should not re-estabish it.

1971 UN General Assembly Resolution supports, for the first time, the desirability of abolishing the death penalty.

1971 Amnesty International convenes an international conference in Stockholm to support abolition of the death penalty.

1972 US Supreme Court rules that the death penalty is unconstitutional as applied in the USA at that time, as it is in violation of the 8th Amendment against 'cruel and unusual punishment'.

1973 Death penalty is abolished in Northern Ireland.

1973 Australian federal parliament abolishes the death penalty, last used in the state of Victoria in 1967.

1976 Canada abolishes the death penalty for all crimes, except treason (abolished 1998).

1976 US Supreme Court rules that the death penalty is constitutional, if safeguards are in place, separating decisions on a prisoner's guilt or innocence and their sentencing.

1977 Executions resume in USA.

1977 Last execution takes place in France – also the last in the European Community (now European Union).

1981 France abolishes the death penalty.

1985 Protocol 6 of the European Convention of Human Rights comes into force whereby all members of the Council of Europe agree to use the death penalty only in times of war and national emergency.

1988 US Supreme Court abolishes capital punishment for people who commit the crime under the age of 16 years.

1989 Amnesty International launches international campaign to abolish the death penalty.

1990 The General Assembly of the Organization of American States takes its first steps to abolish the death penalty in the Americas.

1990 United Nations Convention on the Rights of the Child outlaws capital punishment for people who commit the crime under the age of 18 years.

1991 Second Optional Protocol to the International Covenant on Civil and Political Rights on the total abolition of the death penalty comes into force. By 2006, it has been ratified by 57 countries and signed by a further 33 countries.

2002 US Supreme Court bans execution of 'mentally retarded' adults.

2003 Protocol 13 of the European Convention of Human Rights comes into force, whereby all members of the Council of Europe agree to abolish the death penalty in all circumstances.

2005 UN Resolution 2005/59, sponsored by 81 nations, affirms the right to life and declares that abolition of the death penalty is essential to protect this right.

2005 US Supreme Court abolishes capital punishment for people who commit the crime under the age of 18 years.

2006 Philippines and Moldova abolish the death penalty for all crimes.

Further information

Useful websites include:

**http://www.amnesty.org/ and
http://www.amnestyusa.org/**

Amnesty International – a leading international
campaigner against the death penalty.

http://www.deathpenaltyinfo.org

Death Penalty Information Center – News and
resources for those campaigning against the death
penalty in the US.

http://deathpenaltyinfo.msu.edu/
Death Penalty Information, High School
Curriculum – issues for debate, further information,
interactive maps, case studies, further resources and
links. Entirely US focused.

http://www.prodeathpenalty.com/
Pro-Death Penalty.com – very supportive of the death
penalty, with a combination of legal resources and
appeals from victim's families.
Entirely US focused.

Index

ETHICAL DEBATES

Contents of titles in the series: